SONG OF THE SUN

A celebration of light
in words and images in the year
of the total eclipse of the sun 1999
in Cornwall.

*written and illustrated
by Sheila Jeffries.*

ELDERBERRY BOOKS

In Memory of my parents Kate and Mont Chapman
with gratitude.

*I would like to thank my husband Ted for his love and support;
and my friends for their warmth and encouragement,
particularly Jenny, Joan, Caroline and Shauna.*

Published in 1999, the year of the total eclipse of the sun.
Elderberry Books
St. Keverne, Cornwall. TR12 6QH

ISBN 0 952 8894 6 3

Printed by Westcountry Printing and Publishing
Mullion, Cornwall
Tel: (01326) 241341

SONG OF THE SUN

CONTENTS

And there's another country, I've heard of long ago,
Most dear to them who love her, most great to them that know,
We may not count her armies, we may not see her King
Her fortress is a faithful heart, her pride is suffering;
And soul by soul and silently her shining bounds increase,
And her ways are ways of gentleness and all her paths are peace.

Sir Cecil Spring-Rice

INTRODUCTION by TED JEFFRIES

We live on a quiet vineyard on the Lizard Peninsula, the southernmost part of Cornwall. The Lizard coastline has an atmosphere of expectancy. The sea stretches to the west straight to the Isles of Scilly, the "Isles of the Blessed", and on across the Atlantic to the New World.

The airs come from the west, clean and fresh and clear. History says that from the sea came the Phoenicians, and Jesus with Joseph of Aramithea. What surprises, and what surprises are still to come?

The light is bright and pure, and the sun sinks in to that western sea in glorious colours. Sheila sees the sun in many different ways. It peers through misty veins of light in our woodland walks, it glows on the ripening barley, and you can feel it soaking into the flanks of cows as they lie basking on the hill sides. Frost is so rare that it is exciting when it comes - a sparkling cobweb and a silver sword of grass is all we can enjoy - no icicles.

We see the birds in the sun all the year. The jackdaws always face the rising sun in spring, and rooks gather in regiments to face the setting sun in autumn. Buzzards float in the thermals high up in the sun's rays. Swallows flash blue as they dive through the sunshine, and goldfinches dart and sparkle.

Over the Lizard the sky is high and wide. At night there are no street lights here and the sun is reflected clearly on the moon and Jupiter and Venus. The sky shows a million stars and the milky way is clearly visible.

Living with Sheila's paintings, I find it fascinating to watch how they change in different lights. "WOODLIGHTS" is a dark group of forest trees in ordinary daylight, but in the evening when the lights are switched on, the sun behind the trees bursts into radiant reflected light, and energy seems to stream from it. The huge "CELTIC SUN" is always radiant in every form of light.

Her "FLOWER IN A CAVE" is very personal and always makes me smile and glow with happiness as it tells so much of our story.

The beautiful vista of "CORN INTO FROST" is serene and shows us our way forward into the glowing beauty of light.

*"You never enjoy the world aright, till the sea itself floweth
in your veins, till you are clothed with the heavens,
and crowned with the stars"*

Thomas Traherne

WOODLIGHTS
Acrylic Collage with Holograms 1998

ARTIST'S NOTES - THE DAWN OF AWARENESS

Spring sunlight through bare branches, the stained glass window of the woods, the burning blues of the spring sky latticed with twigs like an underwater forest.

The emerging sparks of life, the nature spirits, the dawning of growth and awareness.

Beyond the branches of our lives the spirit sun blazes forever bright.
Think positive.
Focus on the light.

Our birth is but a sleep and a forgetting
The soul that rises with us, our life's star
Hath had elsewhere its setting
And cometh from afar
And not in utter nakedness ,
But trailing clouds of glory do we come
From God who is our home.

William Wordsworth

THE EMERALD HOUR- SOLAR ECLIPSE 1999

It is not easy
to hear the message in your dreams,
for dreams are cluttered by materialism,
unlike Jacob's ladder, the dream for a thousand years.

You are all being given messages
but few are hearing them.
It is vital that you protect yourself
from noise and traffic.
Seek out the silent places.
Watch the skies
and listen.

One hour of the darkened sun
can change the oversoul of this planet
as it plunges deep into its emerald hour
before the dawning of awakened spirit.
Watch with the sun
as they watched the crucifixion,
the dark hour and then the sunrise.

Watch and pray,
and be amazed.

For, lo, the winter is past, the rain is over and gone.
The flowers appear on earth; the time of the singing bird is come
and the voice of the turtle is heard in our land.

The Bible - Song of Solomon 2. 10

BIRTH OF YELLOW

Acrylic Collage 30x40 ins. 1979

ARTIST'S NOTES - COLOUR HEALING WITH YELLOW

In the month of May in the water meadows, the buttercups take over the earth. They grow so thickly that the land is bathed in the creative energy of the colour yellow, born from the winter months of flood and frost.

Here the colour yellow is rising from the watery blues and whites in response to the sun, a celebration of yellow.

So in our own lives, times of suffering give birth to new awareness, to gratitude and positive thinking.

Yellow is the colour for healing fatigue and depression. You can receive it into your aura by sitting very still in the sunshine or close to yellow flowers or a burning candle flame.

"Let your light so shine before men
that they may see your good works"

Matthew 2 - 16

THE MUM POEM

A meadow of buttercups, a cloth of gold, was the glorious vista from the bedroom where my Mum died. She spent her last days gazing at them and sharing her joy with all who visited her. Even the doctor was made to look at the buttercups, and went on his way smiling.

Mum was a radiant person, a positive thinker, full of fun and kindliness, with an invincible Christian faith. She was a shining light in all our lives, and when she died, Dad asked me to write a poem about her. It is reproduced here in his own script.

Now is the time to share that poem, and say to all those other radiant Mums out there - go on shining - your light will shine in your children, and in their children, whatever traumas they endure. Traumas are part of our life path, part of our learning and growing - but the light, the inner light, the God light, never goes out.

Mum

The spirit shines from your eyes,
brown eyes speaking of sunlight
that shone through a life time.
you have the strength of the earth
and the courage of the wind
you have the gentleness of the summer grass
and the fire of the winter coal
you radiate happiness
people come close to you
like pins to a magnet
clinging to your smile
for they have
no smile
of their own.

Deep in your childhood
the flame burned
the love grew
in your heart
like a tree that knows no winter
you found love
and you treasured it
and from its trunk
grew many branches
touching the lost ones
you gave
courage to.

"Love seeketh not itself to please
Nor for itself hath any care
But for another gives its ease
And builds a Heaven in Hell's despair"

William Blake

FOXGLOVE SUN
Acrylic Collage 18 x 24 ins. 1996

ARTIST'S NOTES - COLOUR HEALING WITH PINK

The Cornish sun shining through the intense pink of foxglove bells. The colour pink is the colour of love, a colour that soothes, invites and welcomes.

Just as there are many shades of pink ranging from palest peach to softest amethyst, so there are many ways of showing love.

Keep the light always in your heart.

When you smile and are very loving the colour pink comes into your aura. Equally you may receive the colour pink from someone who is kind to you.

It is the colour of unconditional love.

THE SILVER TREE

The only darkness is the dark night of the soul
Do not choose this.
Choose to be happy.

Let your happiness burn so bright
that all may feel its glow.
Build from it a shining tree,
its branches stretching to your friends.
The silver tree will bear its leaves,
heart-shaped and silken in the sun,
and when they blow away in shoals of gold,
a thousand words of love will stay
imprinted on the collective consciousness,
the place where all souls link.

You are needed because you can do this.
You are needed because you can love.
And what you will receive
is immense and glorious power
the freedom of inner joy,
which cannot be bought.

THE AURA OF BRITAIN - SOLAR ECLIPSE 1999

The sacred sand
sings of ancient wisdom.
Each grain is programmed, every crystal charged
with all that happened in the Holy Land.

A solar wind shall stir the sand
and scatter it over the earth.
Into each person crystal sparks
shall whisper the voice of God.

Remember Love that through the earth
has nurtured you and given
water and bread and ripened fruit,
energy, wood and clay,
covered your wars with softening grass,
forgiveness, rainbows, flowers,
and threaded the noise of your machines
with golden birdsong.

Aura of Britain, the silver sea,
is fringed with crystal sand,
and crystal salt within the waves
and amethyst on the shore.

Take your prayers to the beaches,
send them into the light.
Thousands will gather to watch the sun
pass through its emerald hour.

And the earth was without form and void;
and darkness was upon the face of the deep. And the
Spirit of God moved upon the face of the waters.
And God said, Let there be light;
and there was light.

Genesis 1

WATERSUN

Acrylic Collage 2 ft. x 3 ft.

ARTIST'S NOTES - HEALING WITH LIGHT

The mid-summer sunrise colours the morning sea with gold. The water is calm. It magnifies the light.

Stretch out your arms and give your whole being to the light as you face the ocean sunrise. A time to be recharged. A time for new beginnings.

A time to pray, and a time to listen.

If you are depressed and stuck in a difficult situation, imagine your life as a dark and dreary room. Open the curtains, let the sun stream in. Clean it up and add a touch of gold. Put all bitterness into a box and burn it. Give up swearing - it pollutes your aura. Speak only beautiful loving words. Your soul is a beautiful shining being - give it permission to shine.

"Our deepest fear is not that we are inadequate. Our deepest fear is that we are powerful beyond measure. It is our light, not our darkness, that most frightens us. We ask ourselves who am I to be brilliant, gorgeous, talented, fabulous? Actually, who are you not to be? You are a child of God. Your playing small doesn't serve the world. There's nothing enlightened about shrinking so that other people won't feel insecure around you. We were all meant to shine, as children do. We were born to make manifest the glory of God that is within us. It's not just in some of us; It's in Everyone! And as we let our own light shine, we unconsciously give other people permission to do the same. As we are liberated from our own fear, our presence automatically liberates others!"

(Nelson Mandela, Inaugural speech, 1994, South Africa.)

WHAT JOB?

Your work has many strands to weave,
to plait with the work of others.
What does work mean to you?
Drudgery? Monotony? Challenge?
Or is it joy?

Your job is not one job,
though it may take six hours of your day.
What you can do in five minutes
with your heart
is also
above all,
your job.

I am busy. I must get on, you say.
But take a moment.
Stop.
Be still.
In this moment your job is to love.

"They are for religion when in rags and contempt,
but I am for him when he walks
in his golden slippers in the sunshine,
and with applause."

John Bunyan

BARLEY SUN
Acrylic Collage 2 ft. x 3 ft. 1996

ARTIST'S NOTES - LETTING GO.

A single ear of barley forming an archway of the sun, a gateway to the world of light. The long whiskers o f the grain make a perfect parabola to compliment the rays of the sun. A celebration of ripened grain, a joint achievement of man and God.

Let us not be afraid to grow old, to stand tall in the light, allow the fruits of wisdom to ripen within us, and then to let go and give back with timeless joy.

AN APPLE

Remember in your spiritual growth
the lesson of the apple.

Here it is, round, ripe, rosy.
Look back
at the way it began.
A meagre speck of green, unobserved
in the love of the blossom.
It spent all summer merrily growing
Content only to grow
to its full size.

Now, at the high peak of its career
it sits in the fruit bowl
only too happy to be eaten, to be of service,
to be no more.
That is humility.

And even to return
beyond its growing point
to be as a seed and start the whole tree
again.

THE BLUE-CURING ORANGE

I went out
and bought an orange,
not to eat,
to look at:
and to hold a planet in my hand.

In this raggle-tailed brickland
I needed a sun-fired fruit
like the golden belly of summer.

Don't laugh at my orange,
it's the droplet brain of the sun
in molecule.

My cupped hands were empty
like a ring without a stone
now they are filled with this orange.

"The kiss of the sun for pardon
The song of the bird for mirth
You are nearer God's heart in the garden
Than anywhere else on earth"

BLUE GRASS SUN (Detail)
Acrylic Collage 12 x 24 ins. 1997

ARTIST'S NOTES - COLOUR HEALING WITH BLUE

On a hazy morning the colour blue is dominant Within its shades discover amazing turquoise and the healing ray of ultramarine leading you back to purest white.

Blue has more resonance than any other colour. Certain blues seem to sing and it is this quality which enhances your spiritual well-being. The darkest depths of blue act very effectively on our ability to trust, and on related illnesses which usually attack the throat area. Wear a blue scarf, or visualise a ring of blue light around the affected area. Blue, white and gold are the protective colours of the Archangel Michael who protects us from evil.

Forget-me-not blue is the colour of forgiveness, and if you want to forgive someone it helps to picture yourself sending them a beam of blue light along with your prayers. Always ask for forgiveness in the name of Jesus. When you forgive, it is YOU who are healed, for you will no longer have to carry the burden of resentment.

The WaterTree

Words from your hands outstretched,
flowers that link in the dark,
through fingers of rock
the water tree flows.

Thought space
is multiple jigsaws.
You cannot
tread through yourself,
your heart
is indexed.
When the rush of numbers fade
you will come to the water tr
for truth.

You will stand
in strong silver
watching
its rushing knots, its white, white hair.

Words from your hands outstretched,
flowers that link in the dark,
and the water tree
like God
has a shining face.

When the rush of number fades
the space between space
is the water tree
on the face of God
that becomes
the sea.

Sheila
Jeffries

THE COLOUR WHITE

Each of you treads a pure white road
a road that crosses time.
Each road is perfect, look ahead
and see who waits for you.
Observe the rocks along the way
and you will find a special one
a rock of glistening white.
Upon this rock be still and wait,
there will I speak to you.

White is the dove, and white my robe,
White is the crystal snow,
White is the salt that purifies
and white the ray that heals.

Why not wear the colour white
and let your aura shine?
Or split the white and wear the gold
The pink, the blue, the jade
and use the colours to create your day,
For colour talks, it talks to you
It whispers to your friends
it reassures, it comforts and it cheers.

Why do you walk in clothes of black
as if to hide your light?
Do you really want to disappear?
Do you really want to creep
along the road of purest white
where angels wait for you?

And not by Eastern windows only,
When daylight comes, comes in the light.
In front the sun climbs slow, how slowly
But Westward look, the land is bright!

Arthur Clough

CORN INTO FROST
Multi-media collage and pastel. 18 x 24 ins.1997

ARTIST'S NOTES - A PICTURE FOR MEDITATION

Barley blue and barley gold. Golden harvest passing into winter. Changing seasons framing the eternal sun. Fire and water, earth and air. Opposites working together to create perfection.

I have used real barley on this picture, from a barley field high on the Cornish cliffs where glimpses of the sea can be seen through the waving golden stalks.

Looking at the light through an opening is a good image for meditation. Close your eyes and imagine yourself walking through into the sunlight.

THE ORANGE FLOWER OF THE FROST

Turned to stone, to marble
by grief and cruelty,
fear and fatigue too deep to feel the sun,
I slept, and a dream was given.

I dreamed of a frozen orchard
with ancient apple trees.
Lichen, moss, and stiff white grass
sparkled with hoary frost.
The air was filled with shining mist,
and out of the ice-locked earth
there grew a flower
before my eyes,
a lily filled with fire.

I gazed in wonder, it grew tall
and opened to the sun.

"I am the flower of love" it said,
"The orange flower of the frost,
A flower that blooms no matter what
In the harshest, hostile place.
A flower that shines with holy fire,
fire of me
of my spirit,
spirit of love.
I will never leave you."

It never did,
and now I am that flower.

FLOWER IN A CAVE
Acrylic collage 18 x 24 ins. 1995

ARTIST'S NOTES - "LOVE CHANGES EVERYTHING"
Before and after flowers - the unloved blue flower drooping and sad with its' face to the earth - the loved flower radiant and fully open to the sun.

Let us love one another. Actively, with compliments and hugs, warmth and forgiveness, and cups of tea and flowers. Your love can help to bring peace on earth.

God is working his purpose out as year succeeds to year
God is working his purpose out and the time is drawing near.
Nearer and nearer draws the time, the time that shall surely be
When the earth shall be filled with the glory of God as the waters
cover the sea.

A.C. Ainger

CELTIC SUN (Detail)

Acrylic collage 4 x 4 ft. 1996

ARTIST'S NOTES - MILLENNIUM SPIRITUALITY

The Celtic cross blended with full spectrum sun light. The sunblaze is divided into four sections: the golds and greens of the plant world with little spirals suggestive of ferns uncurling in the woods. The ultramarine and turquoise from above. From East and West come the rich jades and purples of the Cornish sea with white spirals suggestive of waves.

The octagonal form of the Celtic Cross is a spiritual symbol, the octagon being widely used in sacred architecture.

I regard this picture as a full shining blend of spirituality, old and new, a celebration of what is possible and what is to come in the next millennium when "The earth shall be filled with the glory of God"

HOW THE SUN PAINTINGS CAME INTO BEING

After my art training at Bath Academy of Fine Arts, I didn't pick up a paint brush for eight years!

I am a mystic and my writing and painting is guided from the spirit. In the seventies I spent time in Glastonbury, and worked at perfecting a collage technique suitable for expressing the visions of light which crowded my mind. My fascination with sacred geometry led me to do a series of 30 paintings based on Glastonbury, and all of these are now in private collections.

The first suns were painted on a table in the corner of a very noisy London bedsit. I was guided by Pahiro, a spirit guide who describes himself as the "keeper of the heavenly galleries". He told me to use only spectrum colours, and for me this was a door to creative freedom. In the years at art college I had struggled with the kind of colours we were taught to use - ochre, sepia, terracotta. To me these colours were polluted, depressing and JOYLESS. The pure colours of the rainbow suddenly empowered me to express what I have always known - that God is pure light, and within that light are the seven rays of his teaching.

LOVE, JOY, CREATIVITY, PEACE, FORGIVENESS, WISDOM, TRUTH.

I have always been able to see auras around people, animals and plants. Every living thing is cocooned in celestial light. Painting this light seemed both a privilege and a responsibility, a way of sharing joy, of drawing attention to the light of the world which is always there for us.

That first collection of sun paintings were exhibited in London at the Mall Galleries, the International Arts Centre, Loggia Gallery, and outside London at the Oxford Playhouse Gallery, The Young Gallery, Salisbury, Dillington House Gallery, and finally at the Festival for Mind Body Spirit at Olympia. All except four of these paintings were sold to private collectors and healing centres.

Most artists will tell you that their work is cyclical. There are years of painting and years of not painting. During my years of not painting, I worked as a special needs teacher and a writer of children's fiction. I spent three years studying meditation, colour healing and counselling at a healing centre, and it was here that Pahiro again began appearing to me.

This time it was pastel portraits of spirit guides done in pure spectrum colours on pure white paper, including their radiant auras.

In 1994 I came to live here on the Lizard Peninsula in Cornwall, and with the healing love and encouragement of my beloved husband Ted, I began to paint and write once more, this time in a spacious light filled studio. Pictures queued up in my mind to be painted - doves, angels, flowers, but mostly suns, building up to the solar eclipse 1999.

The paintings are done on heavy duty board because of their depth which is built up from layers of collage. I use carefully graded textured papers, sand, barley, grasses and more recently, reflective material, holograms, beads and stars.

Photographs cannot do justice to these paintings for their texture catches the light in many different ways. It is possible for a blind person to enjoy the paintings through touch. Many people have found the sun paintings ideal for meditation, for healing sanctuaries, hospitals and places where light and colour are needed.

Through this time of producing a new collection of paintings, I have re-discovered my spiritual path. I have been constantly guided to 'build bridges' between New Age Spirituality and the Churches, and both are very dear to my heart. That is what the largest painting, CELTIC SUN, is about - one light, one church, one people, radiant in the beams of God's love. A vision and a prayer for the millenium.

Sheila Jeffries 1998.

AN ANGEL IN STONE

Artists are born, not made.

It is VISION that drives us to create - the skill is secondary.

As a child I watched my dad, Mont Chapman, create amazing sculptures from wood and stone. He never had an art lesson in his life. But he had vision.

"I'll bet you can't carve an angel from this stone gate post." A friend challenged him, back in the 1930's. He did. It was as if the angel waited inside the stone to be discovered, a perfect angel, gentle faced with curving wings and praying hands. That small stone angel is now on the windowsill in Woolavington Church, Somerset.

Carving became Dad's life long hobby, and his sculptures of owls, dolphins, comorants and monkey faces can still be found in many Somerset homes. He had no studio.

His greatest work in wood was the statue of St. Joseph, now in St. Joseph's Church, Bridgwater. I watched it appear, chip by chip from a block of mahogany. It took him six months, working in a freezing cold garage among the old oil cans and spanners. It was truly a labour of love. Dad also practised calligraphy, and when my book of poetry WATERSUN was published, he took one of my poems to his heart and wrote it out in beautiful script.

Dad's influence on my life has been fantastic. Not only was he a born artist, but he had the gift of prophecy. He didn't talk much, but when he did, people listened, and his words always came true. He guided me with gentle love, patience and immense wisdom.

And he always signed his letters KPO - Keep plodding on!

St Joseph

Spirit of truth and love
Life-giving, holy Dove
Speed forth thy flight.
Move on the waters' face
Bearing the lamp of grace
And in earth's darkest place
Let there be light!

J. Marriott.